A HUMMINGBIRD ON MY BALCONY

ISABELLE GROC

ORCA BOOK PUBLISHERS

This is Noah. He has just moved into a new apartment on the 22nd floor with his parents. To celebrate the holidays Noah's family installed lights on the balcony railing. The little boy was happy to see the lights among the other high-rise buildings, so his parents decided to keep them up for a little longer after the holidays.

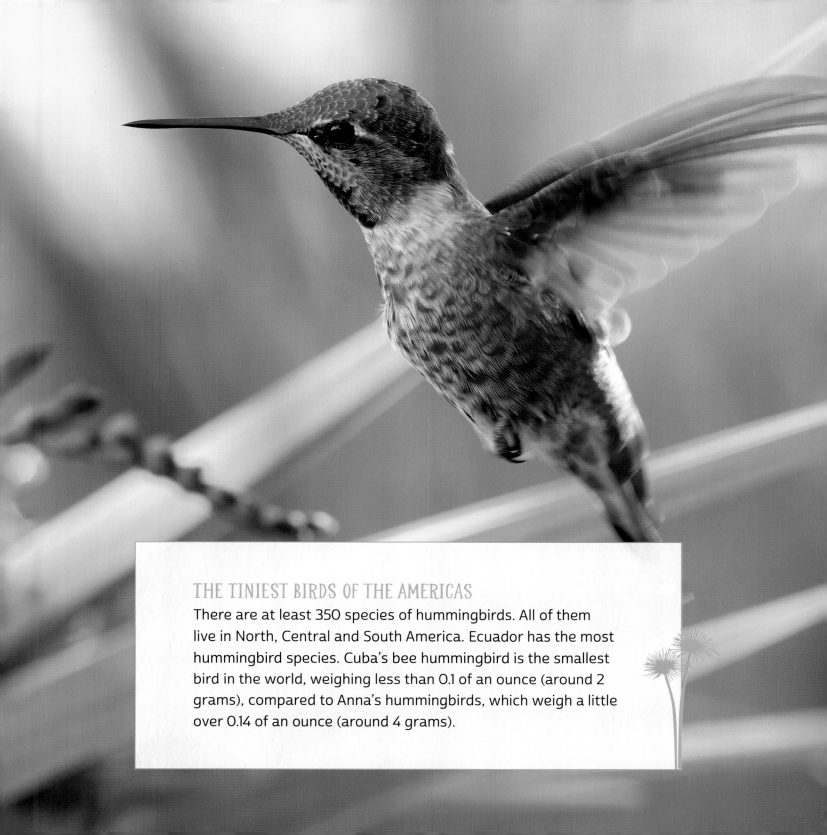

THE TINIEST BIRDS OF THE AMERICAS

There are at least 350 species of hummingbirds. All of them live in North, Central and South America. Ecuador has the most hummingbird species. Cuba's bee hummingbird is the smallest bird in the world, weighing less than 0.1 of an ounce (around 2 grams), compared to Anna's hummingbirds, which weigh a little over 0.14 of an ounce (around 4 grams).

One day in February, a tiny, colorful bird became very interested in the lights. It was exciting to have a surprise guest from the sky. The family discovered the balcony visitor was a female Anna's hummingbird. Noah didn't know much about hummingbirds, just that when they fly, their wings make a humming sound. That's why some people call them hummers.

THE METAL SINGER

Hummingbirds make sound when the feathers of their wings or tail vibrate against the air. Their call is a kind of metallic *cheep-cheep-cheep*. Hummers can be quite loud, especially when they are defending their feeding territory. Male Anna's hummingbirds, more vocal than most hummingbirds, sing a dry, scratchy, buzzy song while perched.

Noah noticed a fuzzy little platform on the balcony and realized that the hummingbird was busy building a nest. Why would the tiny bird choose to raise a family here, high above the streets of the city, among the tall concrete buildings? Noah learned that's because Anna's hummingbirds have adapted to live near people.

LANDED IMMIGRANT

Anna's hummingbird populations have grown in number, and they are now found in more places. That's thanks to the exotic flowers that bloom in different seasons and the nectar feeders that people provide for them in gardens year-round. In the early 1900s Anna's hummingbirds mostly lived in central and southern California, but they began to move northward and eastward. Anna's hummers can now be found as far north as British Columbia and even into Alaska. They are able to survive cold nights because they go into a special hibernation-like state called torpor.

CHAMPIONS OF FLIGHT

No other bird can match the aerial acrobatics of hummingbirds. They can fly forward, backward and sideways. They are the only birds that can hover in one place for long periods. Rufous hummingbirds are known for their extraordinary flight skills. They make one of the longest migratory journeys of any bird in the world, when it's measured by how far they travel compared to their size.

Over several days the hummingbird went back and forth, bringing small downy feathers and plant pieces to make her nest. Noah loved watching the hummingbird fly. It reminded him of a helicopter. The lights on the balcony were a perfect spot to protect a hummingbird family from the wind and the rain and keep them well hidden from predators. But it seemed like such a precarious spot, so high up. Noah was worried the nest would fall down with the first gust of wind.

A master seamstress, the hummingbird used threads of spider silk, nature's strongest glue, to hold the tiny home together and secure it to the foundation. She shaped the nest into a cup by stamping her feet, rotating her body and smoothing the outer edge with her chin. For finishing touches, she added tiny bits of bark, twigs, lichen, leaves and moss to the outside of the nest to keep it well hidden.

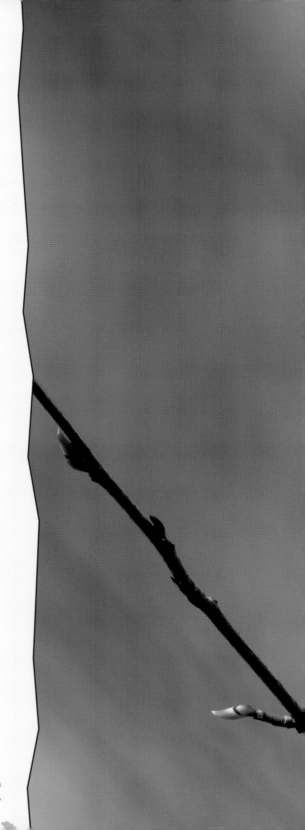

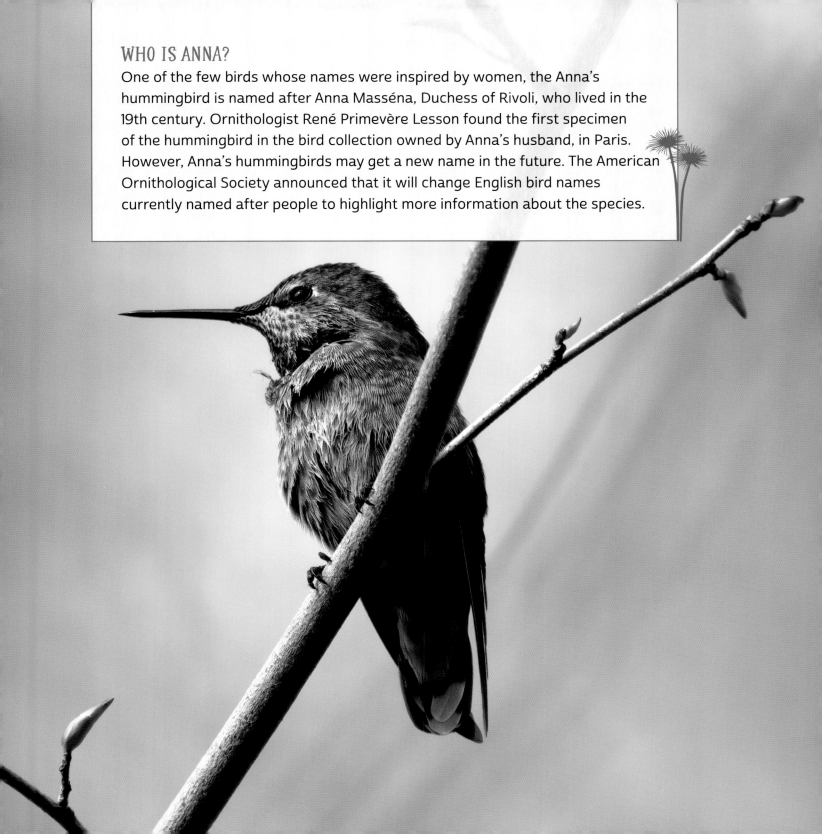

WHO IS ANNA?

One of the few birds whose names were inspired by women, the Anna's hummingbird is named after Anna Masséna, Duchess of Rivoli, who lived in the 19th century. Ornithologist René Primevère Lesson found the first specimen of the hummingbird in the bird collection owned by Anna's husband, in Paris. However, Anna's hummingbirds may get a new name in the future. The American Ornithological Society announced that it will change English bird names currently named after people to highlight more information about the species.

SHINY FEATHERS, FLYING COLORS

Hummingbirds have been called flying jewels because of how colorful they are. The female Anna's hummingbird has a green back and iridescent specks of pink and red on her throat while the male has a bright reddish-pink crown and throat (called a gorget, after the metal collar a knight in armor would wear to protect his throat). The male's shiny feathers seem to change color in different light. The bird turns his head from side to side as he sings, flashing his gorget to attract females or intimidate rivals.

As his family settled into their new apartment, Noah watched the little hummingbird make her own home. He knew that it was important not to bother the hummingbird while she was setting up her house. From building a nest to incubating eggs and caring for the babies, parenting is entirely the responsibility of the mother.

A tiny white egg the size of a jelly bean appeared in the nest. The next day, the hummingbird laid another egg. Day after day Noah watched her sit on the eggs, taking only short breaks to feed herself. She seemed so calm, oblivious to the city lights and traffic sounds.

THREATS TO HUMMINGBIRDS

The nesting sites, winter homes and migratory corridors of hummingbirds are threatened by human activities. The warming climate and extreme weather events can destroy the nectar-producing plants that hummers depend on for food. The loss of wetlands and ponds also means there are fewer insects for hummingbirds to eat. People sometimes use chemicals to get rid of insects they don't want, and this too reduces the food available to hummingbirds. In urban areas the tiny birds face many risks, including being caught by cats, crashing into windows, drinking from dirty feeders and being hit by cars.

IF YOU FIND AN INJURED OR ORPHANED HUMMINGBIRD

A mother Anna's hummingbird does not abandon a nest unless something happens to her. She may be hit by a car, for example, or caught by a cat. In cases like that, the chicks are left to fend for themselves. If you suspect a nest has been abandoned, watch it from a distance for at least an hour, sometimes more, to be sure the mother is not returning. Don't look away, as she is quick! Feedings can be infrequent at some stages of the chicks' development. Contact your local wildlife rehabilitation center for help if you think the mother is gone. Never try to nurse or raise a hummingbird or any other bird on your own. They are delicate creatures that can be easily injured if handled.

One day Noah came home from school and told his family he had thought of a name for the hummingbird. He was going to call her Vita. Neighbors and friends wanted to know all about the hummingbird. Would she succeed in raising a family in this unexpected home?

Later, as Vita was sitting on the nest, there was a storm with high winds. Noah worried that the nest might fall. Should he pile pillows beneath it? But Vita was strong, and the spider silk she had used to form the nest never failed.

The family counted 17 days after the first egg appeared in the nest until the babies finally hatched! At first Vita sat on the chicks to keep them warm, only leaving the nest to find food. Noah thought the babies looked so fragile, snuggled inside the tiny, cozy nest.

A BIG APPETITE

Hummingbirds like this juvenile male Rufous hummingbird feed on sugar found in the nectar of flowers. Sometimes they also drink tree sap from wells drilled by sapsuckers. They need protein, too, so they eat lots of small insects and tiny spiders. Hummers need tons of food because they constantly burn energy while on the move. They eat nearly twice their weight or more each day. Hummingbirds have long tongues shaped like forks that help them lick up the nectar from flowers at high speed—they can lick 15 to 20 times per second.

Noah watched how Vita fed the babies. When Vita returned to the nest with nectar and tiny bugs, the babies tipped up their heads and opened their mouths. Vita put her bill deep into the throat of one baby, pumping her neck muscles as she regurgitated the insect mixture. "Yuk!" Noah said. "I would not like to be fed like that!"

The babies were well protected in the nest when Vita was off looking for food. Noah called them Enzo and Tom, after two of his favorite characters in a book about two male birds who noticed an abandoned egg in a nest and decided to adopt and raise the baby bird themselves.

THE POLLINATOR JOB

These two Rufous hummingbirds—like any other hummingbird species—are attracted to nectar-rich flowers by their bright colors. The birds have large eyes and excellent vision. They can see a whole range of colors that are invisible to humans, including ultraviolet colors. Hummingbirds do more than get nectar from flowers. Like insects, they play an important role in transferring pollen from one flower to another. Many plants require pollination to make seeds. When a hummingbird puts its bill into a flower, some of the pollen sticks to its head and body. The hummingbird then carries this pollen from flower to flower. On average, hummingbirds visit between 1,000 and 2,000 flowers every day.

The babies grew quickly. Even though the nest was designed to stretch as the nestlings grew, it was getting tight for them. At about two weeks old, Enzo and Tom were almost as big as their mother. They started to sit on the edge of the nest and began to exercise their wings.

One morning, 21 days after hatching, one of the youngsters left the nest, launching into an awkward first flight. Its sibling enjoyed the comfort of the nest for one last night, preening its feathers. It flew away the next morning. And then the whole family was gone. The nestlings wouldn't be on their own right away, though. The mother would continue to feed them for a few more days as they strengthened their wings and learned how to find food on their own.

BIG HEARTS

Hummingbirds have the largest hearts (relative to body size) in the entire animal kingdom, and their heartbeat is fast—up to 1,200 beats per minute.

A HUMMINGBIRD NEVER FORGETS

The hummingbird has an amazing memory. Thanks to its large hippocampus—the area of the brain responsible for learning and memory—a hummer can make a mental map of previous feeding locations in its home territory and along migration routes. What's more, a special part of the brain involved in motion detection helps it maintain its position in space while hovering and during high-speed flight.

Noah felt sad and happy at the same time. He was proud that his new home had provided a safe place for the hummingbird mother to raise a family. After the young birds left, he often wondered how they were doing. The following spring he kept an eye on the balcony, hoping that Vita or one of her babies would come back to start a new family, but no one showed up. Would he ever see them again? Another year went by before a hummingbird arrived on their balcony again. Noah was very excited when it built another nest in the exact same spot. When the new babies, Marmalade and Rose, eventually flew away, Noah was sure they would be back one day. The hummingbirds were family.

LIVING WITH HUMMINGBIRDS

You can take a few simple actions to create a safe home for hummingbirds.

- Plant a variety of native, colorful, nectar-rich flowers on your patio, in your back garden or on your apartment balcony.
- Add high perches for the birds to rest on and shrubs to serve as cover for nesting and protection from the weather.
- Install a moving water feature.
- Install a pond.

- Hang a feeder filled with sugar water (1/4 cup white sugar dissolved in 1 cup boiled water). Be sure it's hung high enough to be safe from cats. Feeders must be hand washed in hot water (with a small amount of vinegar in the water) and refilled every two to three days. Use a feeder heater in the winter, as hummingbirds depend on your feeder when it gets cold.
- Reduce window collisions by making glass more visible to the birds.

AUTHOR'S NOTE

I have always had a special love for hummingbirds, especially Anna's hummingbirds. They are an enchanting window into the natural world, accessible to anyone who takes the time to notice them. With their dazzling colors and incredible speed, they have the surprising power to slow us down. Anna's hummingbirds thrive alongside people in urban areas. Usually they build their nests on tree branches, but in cities they take advantage of unusual nesting spots like plant hooks, outdoor lights, electrical wires and patio decorations.

Even though Anna's hummingbirds live close to us, their nests are well camouflaged and can be difficult to find. When I started working on this project, I asked people on social media if they knew of nests in urban parks or in their backyards. I am very grateful for the incredible support of the scientists, naturalists, photographers, homeowners and friends who helped me identify nest locations.

I met people like Noah and his family who shared their lives with hummingbirds and allowed me to visit them and document nests near their homes for several weeks. I realized how much comfort and joy the birds brought with every whirr of their wings to anyone who was lucky enough to have these visitors make a home in their backyards.

Like the strong spider silk that holds hummingbird nests together, these birds bind communities together and bring out the best in us. They are a reminder of the power of nature in our lives and why it is so essential to protect it.

To hummingbirds and the people who help protect these endlessly captivating birds.

Published in Canada and the United States in 2025 by Orca Book Publishers.
orcabook.com

Library and Archives Canada Cataloguing in Publication
Title: A hummingbird on my balcony / Isabelle Groc.
Names: Groc, Isabelle, author, photographer.
Identifiers: Canadiana (print) 20240371704 | Canadiana (ebook) 20240371712 |
ISBN 9781459831667 (hardcover) | ISBN 9781459831674 (PDF) | ISBN 9781459831681 (EPUB)
Subjects: LCSH: Hummingbirds—Juvenile literature. | LCSH: Hummingbirds—Life cycles—Juvenile literature. |
LCSH: Human-animal relationships—Juvenile literature. | LCGFT: Picture books.
Classification: LCC QL696.A558 G76 2025 | DDC j598.7/64—dc23

Library of Congress Control Number: 2024938024

Summary: This nonfiction picture book tells the true story of an Anna's hummingbird that built a nest and
raised its babies on a family's balcony in the city. Illustrated with photographs throughout.

Orca Book Publishers is committed to reducing the consumption of nonrenewable resources in the production of our books.
We make every effort to use materials that support a sustainable future.

Orca Book Publishers gratefully acknowledges the support for its publishing programs provided by the following agencies: the Government of Canada,
the Canada Council for the Arts and the Province of British Columbia through the BC Arts Council and the Book Publishing Tax Credit.

Cover and interior images by Isabelle Groc.
Author photo by Sam Trull.
Design by Rachel Page.
Edited by Kirstie Hudson.

Printed and bound in South Korea.

28 27 26 25 • 1 2 3 4

ISABELLE GROG is a writer, wildlife photographer, filmmaker and speaker who focuses on environmental issues, wildlife natural history and conservation, endangered species and the changing relationships between people and their environments. Her stories and photographs have appeared in numerous publications, and her wildlife films have been shown in communities and festivals around the world. Isabelle is the author of *Gone Is Gone*, *Conservation Canines* and *Sea Otters* in the Orca Wild series. Born in the South of France, with family roots in Spain, Isabelle now lives in Vancouver.